JIM THORPE

By Robert Reising

DILLON PRESS, INC.

MINNEAPOLIS, MINNESOTA

Dillon Press, Inc., 500 South Third Street
Minneapolis, Minnesota 55415

Printed in the United States of America

Library of Congress Cataloging in Publication Data

Reising, Robert.
   Jim Thorpe.
   SUMMARY: A biography of the Oklahoma Indian
who won fame for his all-around athletic excellence, but
was plagued with personal difficulties throughout his life.
   1. Thorpe, Jim, 1888-1953 — Juvenile literature.
[1. Thorpe, Jim, 1888-1953.   2. Athletes.   3. Indians of
North America — Biography]   I. Title.
GV697.T5R44   796'.092'4   [B]   [92]   74-13150
ISBN 0-87518-076-0

ON THE COVER:
Jim Thorpe at the
Carlisle Indian School

The author wishes to acknowledge the
members of the staff of the Robeson
County, North Carolina, Public Library,
and especially Mrs. A. T. Parmele, its
Director, who provided invaluable
assistance in the researching of this book.

JIM THORPE

Fifty years after the death of Black Hawk, the greatest
warrior of the Sac and Fox tribe, his great-great-grandson
was born — Jim Thorpe, one of the greatest athletes
of all time. Even in his early years, two facets of
Jim Thorpe's life stand out: personal excellence in
athletics, and an unfair share of personal tragedies,
beginning with the death of his twin brother at age
eight. In 1912, Jim Thorpe became the only person ever
to win both the Olympic Pentathlon and Decathlon
events — only to have his honors stripped from him
over a technicality. He went on to achieve success in
both professional baseball and football. Although he
faced family deaths, two divorces, and an alcohol
problem, Jim Thorpe was a champion and a fighter
throughout his life. Deservedly, he is remembered with
respect and affection both as an athlete and a great man.

Contents

CHAPTER I

Bright Path

Sir, you are a man; so am I. But fortune has placed us in different circumstances. Your people are stronger than mine. You can dictate your terms. I am your prisoner, and must submit, but I am still a man, the same as you.

So spoke Ma-ka-tai-me-she-kia-kiak, known to the white men as Black Hawk, and the greatest warrior ever to represent the Sac and Fox tribe. The year was 1832, and Black Hawk was speaking to Andrew Johnson, the seventh president of the United States. The Indian warrior was surrendering to the white men, but neither he nor any other Sac and Fox Indians were about to give up their dignity and their pride. It was impossible to break the spirit of this leader or his people.

Nearly two hundred years before, the Sac — the "people of the yellow earth" — and the Fox — the "red earth people" — had lived as separate tribes in Canada and on the shores of the Great Lakes. Both were Algonquian-speaking peoples, and both lived in permanent villages. Their houses were long, bark-covered lodges large enough to hold several families. Every year the tribes planted such crops as beans, corn, and squash near their villages. After harvesting their vegetables, the people would set out on long hunting trips to search for buffalo, which provided them with meat and hides. When winter arrived, the people would camp wherever they happened to be, but they would return to their villages in the spring to begin planting their crops again.

In the early 1700s, the Sac and Fox were pushed toward the south by the French and the Chippewas. There they joined forces and formed a confederacy to fight off their common enemies. Some of them settled in what is now northern Illinois, and others went west of the Mississippi River. Later, many Sac and Fox settled along the beautiful Missouri River.

By the time Black Hawk was born in 1767, the Sac and Fox alliance had grown very strong, and the tribe claimed much of the land in what are now Illinois, Wisconsin, and Missouri. Before 1804, the Sac and Fox fought with other tribes, such as the Cherokees and Osages, but they were not threatened by the white men.

In their fights with other tribes, Black Hawk soon earned the full respect of his people because of his achievements in battle. At fifteen years of age, he led a war party to defeat fierce Osage Indians. Two years later, he was a key figure in his tribe's bloody but successful battle against the Cherokees, a hundred of whom lay dead after the fight.

At home, Black Hawk became a champion in sports. As a youth, he was slender and quick, and once he had gained the full growth of manhood, he proved to be the best athlete in his tribe. No one could surpass him as a runner, jumper, wrestler, and swimmer, and few warriors dared to try.

Black Hawk,
Sac and Fox leader

In 1804, a group of Sac and Fox living along the Missouri River gave up to the whites a large part of their lands in Wisconsin, Illinois, and Missouri. The other Sac and Fox were furious. During the next years, tensions increased between those who signed the treaty and those who did not. There was also much hostility toward the white men. In 1831, Black Hawk tried to rally all of his people and get them to remain in Illinois in defiance of the white men's orders to leave. Black Hawk described his feelings about the land in his autobiography:

> My reason teaches me that that land cannot be sold.
> The Great Spirit gave it to his children to live upon,
> and cultivate, as far as is necessary for their subsis-
> tence, they have the right to the soil . . . . Nothing can
> be sold, but such things as can be carried away.

He pleaded with the Sac and Fox to stand against the white men who, in his words, "came year after year, to cheat his countrymen and take their lands." Thus began the Black Hawk War of 1831-1832, which ended with the defeat of the Sac and Fox by the U.S. Army and the imprisonment of Black Hawk. The warrior was later paroled, and he died in 1838.

After his passing, the tribe moved to what is now Iowa, which they claimed as their territory after driving out the Sioux Indians. They lived there until a series of settlements with the white men, ending in 1861, gave the whites all Sac and Fox lands in Iowa, Nebraska, and Kansas. Later, some members of the tribe purchased with their own money an area of land in Iowa, where many have remained to this day. Others lived on land in Kansas and Oklahoma that was set aside for them by the U.S. government. For many years after losing their power to the whites, the tribe resisted the civilization brought by their conquerors. They were, certainly, among the last Indians to accept the new ways.

Fifty years after the death of Black Hawk, his great-great-grandson was born, a child destined to become even more famous than the great warrior. On May 28, 1888, in a simple log cabin near what is now Prague, Oklahoma, Jim Thorpe entered the world, one of twin boys born to Charlotte View and Hiram Thorpe. He was christened James Francis Thorpe, but his parents also gave him an Indian Name, Wa-Tho-Huck, meaning "Bright Path." They somehow sensed that this infant would one day make a name for himself as his great-great-grandfather had done. And it was a bright path that the infant was eventually to follow — a path so bright, in fact, that he was to become respected throughout the entire world. Jim Thorpe brought glory to himself, to his nation, and to all people who love sport and competition. He stands as a shining example of what the human body can do when muscle and mind aim at perfection. Black Hawk would indeed have been pleased with him.

Jim was always proud of his fearless ancestor and of his rich Indian background. As an adult, he often spoke of his admiration for Black Hawk, and on one occasion said, "I am no more proud of my career as an athlete than I am of the fact that I am a direct descendent of that noble warrior."

Jim's mother, Charlotte View, was from the Potawatomi tribe, which originally lived in the region around the Great Lakes and later moved to Oklahoma. Her people were called "The Firemakers" because of their skill with flints and other fire-making tools, and they also were respected because of the quality of their crafts. Although one-fourth French, Jim's mother was proudest of her Indian ancestry, and she introduced Jim to it while he was still quite young. The Potawatomi had much to be proud of, he soon found out, just as the Sac and Fox, his father's tribe, had good reason to be respected. Evenings of Jim's first years were filled with tales about the two tribes with their long and noble histories.

"Big Hiram," Jim's father, was half Irish and half Sac and Fox. He was a huge man who liked to have plenty of elbow room. Around 1880, before Jim was born, he had left the Iowa reservation where he had been living for a 160-acre farm in Oklahoma that had been provided by the government. This was so large a spread that he was kept busy working it from dawn to dusk. But once the chores of the day were completed, Big Hiram had time for those activities he loved just as much as he loved his freedom — hunting, fishing, running, jumping, riding, climbing, and wrestling. He enjoyed anything that tested him physically, and like Black Hawk, he had a flair for competition and a desire for excellence. He, too, had few equals. No one in the Prague area could defeat him in sports — he was the local champion. His son was proud of his father's achievements and he tried to be the best in similar contests among boys his own age. Jim Thorpe came from a family of champions, and early in life he dedicated himself to being one, too.

But the large farm demanded more work than it allowed play. Just as soon as he was able to help, Jim had to handle a share of the many chores. Running errands and tending and feeding the livestock were his first assignments, and while he preferred games with his brothers or sisters, he performed his duties without complaining. Fortunately, some of the responsibilities of the farm were a mixture of work and play, and Jim looked forward to these tasks more than to any others. The family had to rely on hunting and fishing to supply much of their food, and Jim eagerly helped out as soon as he was old enough. Big Hiram was an excellent teacher, and it did not take him long to realize that Jim was an especially interested and able student, one with more promise than his other sons.

The search for bear, deer, and rabbit often took them far from the farm for days, even weeks, at a time. Jim soon became familiar with traps, snares, bows and arrows, and guns. By the time he had reached his seventh birthday he had participated in many hunting and fishing trips, and shortly after reaching his tenth year he had killed his first deer with a rifle shot. Soon after this, when Jim was about eleven years old, he first tried breaking a colt. By the time he was fifteen, he had the confidence to announce, "I never met a wild one that I could not catch, saddle, and ride." Jim truly enjoyed almost every activity that made demands upon his fast-growing body.

Naturally, Big Hiram and his wife would not allow their children to grow up uneducated, so at the age of six, in the company of his twin brother Charlie, Jim was sent to the Sac and Fox reservation school, which was twenty-three miles from the farm. Because of the distance, the twins had to live at the school, returning to their home only on holidays, during summers, and occasionally for a weekend.

Jim did not mind, though, for while he would rather be around Big Hiram and the farm, the school was not an unpleasant place. He and Charlie were very close, and they both joined many of the same school activities. There were games as well as books, sports as well as studies, and Jim came to enjoy them all. And, of course, whenever he met a dull or a boring moment, Jim could look forward to a holiday, weekend, or summer visit home. Time flew, and Jim grew both physically and mentally.

But too soon, the first of many personal tragedies struck. Charlie caught a cold that held on; soon it turned into pneumonia and he became feverish. No powerful drugs or well-trained doctors were available to treat him, and despite the efforts of his friends and family, he died late in 1896. Jim felt the loss greatly; at eight years of age, it was difficult for him to understand and accept the passing of a brother who had shared just about every waking hour with him. But though his sorrow was strong, it was silent. As a boy, and later as an adult, he always refused to show his feelings. He preferred to mourn quietly, in the tradition of Black Hawk and his other noble ancestors.

But the death of his twin left its mark. Jim refused to return to the reservation school, preferring, he told Big Hiram, to work with his parents back on the farm. He argued that he was needed to help with the chores; the farm work was demanding, and he could do a man's job. But his father would have none of Jim's arguments. Education was important, very important, he told his son, and he was going to make sure Jim attended school. When Jim saw that Big Hiram was not about to budge, he gave up his argument and unwillingly returned to school.

Yet is was not the same place. With Charlie gone it was different, not half so cheerful or fun filled. The other Indian boys were friendly, but they could not replace his twin; no one could. There was only one thing to do — return to the farm and persuade Big Hiram to reconsider. Jim thought his father would surely change his mind once he saw how determined his son was. So, one morning not long after Charlie's death, with a hearty breakfast under his belt, Jim started for home. Sometimes walking, often trotting, usually running, Jim's slender but strong legs quickly carried him the twenty-three miles. But his plans failed. Big Hiram greeted him coolly, told him that he could be just as determined as his young son, and turned him around and accompanied him back to the school.

The Thorpe home
in Yale, Oklahoma

Jim was unwilling to stay. Not two minutes after his father had left him at the school, he took off for home again. Using a shortcut unknown to Big Hiram, he eliminated five miles from the long trip and arrived at the farm moments before his father did. When Big Hiram saw Jim at home for the second time on the same day, he was very surprised, but he was determined that Jim should be in a school. If Jim would not remain at the reservation school, he would have to attend one farther away, in another state. Though he didn't know of many schools, it so happened that Big Hiram had heard of one that he thought ideal for his stubborn son. Haskell Institute in Lawrence, Kansas, was hundreds of miles from the Thorpe farm. Not even Jim's strong legs could run or walk that distance. Equally important, it was (and still is) an all-Indian school with a solid reputation. Big Hiram was confident that Jim would feel comfortable there and receive a good education.

Thus, when he was only eight years old, Jim left his native state and was enrolled at Haskell. He adjusted to the new school quickly, and his stay in Lawrence was both long and pleasant. He enjoyed his studies, his new environment, and the many friends he quickly made.

First among those friends was Chauncey Archiquette, the school's athletic hero. Jim was practically his shadow, so impressed was he by the skillful Indian's abilities in football and baseball. Jim had never known those sports while in Oklahoma, but here, thanks to Archiquette, he saw and played them regularly. And the more Jim participated, the better he became.

Archiquette was a good friend and an ideal coach for Jim. He did not object to the dozens of questions Jim asked about football and baseball. Because he was a superior player of each sport and sensed that Jim could become the same, he passed on many tips that Jim was able to use. But more helpful than any other advice were the words which Archiquette repeated time and time again: "Try it yourself! And practice it a lot!"

Jim did practice long and hard, and he slowly developed those skills that were to serve him so well later in life. No doubt, Jim would have finished at Haskell if a frightening report had not reached him there in 1900. Word came to the campus that Big Hiram lay dying of a gunshot wound in Oklahoma. No one knew who first circulated the rumor, but everyone agreed that it should not reach Jim — he was too young to be of help during so serious a family crisis and would only be in the way if he were to return to the farm.

At the small school, however, it was difficult to control the spread of rumors. Jim soon heard about Big Hiram and his immediate reaction was to race to the local railroad station, where he boarded a freight which he thought would travel near his home in just a few hours. Time was important, he knew, and he wanted to get to his father's side as quickly as possible.

But Jim had acted too quickly. Just a few minutes after boarding it, he sensed the train was traveling in the wrong direction. Again he wasted no time. He hurled himself from the speeding boxcar and, after tumbling and rolling for what he thought were hours, came to rest a short distance from the tracks. His body was badly bruised, his muscles ached, and his left ankle could hardly support any weight at all, but he quickly hopped to his feet again.

With his father near death, there was no time for babying himself. Jim had to get to Oklahoma in a hurry.

And he did. In two weeks, traveling fast and eating little, Jim covered the 250 miles separating Lawrence from his home. The trip took every ounce of his energy, but once he saw his father he knew that it was worth all he had put into it. His father was not near death; in fact, he was on his feet, as alive as ever. Though several weeks earlier he had suffered a serious arm injury in a hunting accident and he still had to use a sling, he was rapidly getting back his full strength and vitality. Jim could see that Big Hiram was soon to be the best athlete in the Prague area again.

Jim's joy was short-lived. Within days of his return to the family farm, Charlotte View was confined to her bed, a victim of blood poisoning. Like Jim's brother Charlie, Charlotte was not treated by modern medicines or well-prepared physicians, and she quietly passed away.

Her death was deeply felt by all whom she left behind. Jim had lost two of his family in four years, one his twin and best friend, the other his devoted mother. This was very difficult for the twelve-year-old. Although there were no public displays of emotion, he was fast coming to realize that life was not without its pains, that it provided problems as well as pleasures.

A return to Haskell was now out of the question, at least for the present. Jim knew that Big Hiram needed his family around him to help. Thus began a four-year period in which Jim lived with and helped his father, and also attended a recently opened reservation school only three miles from the farm. It was a period of studies and chores

broken only by the games in which Jim regularly participated, often with his father, and by two unusual happen-
ings.

The first resulted from a beating that Big Hiram was
forced to give Jim because of his refusal to obey his father.
Jim later admitted that the punishment was just, but at the
time he thought otherwise. With both his pride and his
bottom hurt, he stormed off the farm, determined to prove
that he could get along on his own. One day led into
another, and before he returned to the Prague area, months
had passed and he had performed various odd jobs in
faraway Texas. This did indeed prove that he was a cou-
rageous and capable young man. When Big Hiram saw him
again, he was quietly proud of his son, for Jim was becom-
ing an adult.

The second unusual happening was perhaps less dra-
matic, but it held even greater significance for Jim. Late
in 1903, a traveling superintendent from Carlisle, Pennsylvania, came by chance into the Prague area in search
of students for the Indian school in his city. He spoke with
Jim, learned that he was interested in one of the trades
available at the school, and signed him up right away. Jim
was to report to the campus early in 1904. As he said
good-bye to the visitor from Pennsylvania, little did he
realize that his whole life was about to change. The bright
path that had been predicted for him at birth was to take
on added glow in the years immediately ahead.

CHAPTER II

Carlisle

When Jim entered the Carlisle school just months before his sixteenth birthday, he and Carlisle had one important thing in common: neither was well-known. But in his eight years there, Jim was good for the school, for he helped to make it respected throughout the world. And the school was good for Jim — it provided him with the last part of his schooling, and it allowed and encouraged him to play sports. Jim's youngest daughter later said that during her father's stay on campus, "the athletic feats of the Carlisle Indians were trumpeted all over the world."

The Carlisle school, in the beautiful Cumberland Valley of Pennsylvania, represented the dream-come-true of Lt. Richard Henry Pratt, a man who had made a name for himself both in the Civil War and in the Indian campaigns of 1874-1876. It was the belief of Lieutenant Pratt that the American Indians could benefit from and contribute to American life if they were given solid educational opportunities. Thousands of people disagreed, crying, "Indians can't learn. They're just savages." But the veteran soldier refused to be discouraged. For years he pounded on doors and desks, in Washington and elsewhere, determined to get a campus for the hundreds of young Indians he wished to educate.

Finally, in 1879, the United States government rewarded his efforts, and let him use the run-down and abandoned army barracks at Carlisle. They were in poor condition, but to Lieutenant Pratt they were ideal. With a little luck and a lot of hard work, they could be made, he knew, into a school of national fame. But never in his wildest dreams did he imagine that, thanks to the athletic skills of young men like Jim, the old army post would one day become famous the world over.

So, when Jim arrived in 1904, the school was really only at a beginning. And Jim himself was hardly a likely candidate for fame. He was just a shade over five feet tall and weighed only 110 pounds. In fact, he very much resembled the eighty-two boys and girls who had made up the school's first class in the late fall of 1879. But he grew and adjusted quickly. He had been away from Oklahoma before, and he knew how to adjust to new surroundings.

Within two months after he arrived, his maturity received its toughest test. One day, a teacher quietly called him aside and told him that Big Hiram had died days earlier of the same illness that had taken his mother. Once again, Jim mourned quietly. There were no public cries, for he kept all his tears in his heart. But the pain he felt was even stronger than any before. The three people he loved most — his twin, his mother, and his father — had all departed. The family ranch was now more a house than a home. Jim felt very much alone in the world.

As time went on, he was always friendly with his classmates at Carlisle, but he never became really close with any one of them. Later, Jim would be a famous and popular man, but he would find few relationships as close as those he had had with his twin and his parents. He would remain a loner throughout most of his life.

During his second term and for most of the next two years, as part of his school program, Jim worked away from the campus at a variety of paying jobs in Pennsylvania. The first one, which paid five dollars a month, was as a cook in a private home. Jim disliked this job very much — first, because the family treated him like a slave; second, because he preferred the outdoors. As soon as possible, he changed jobs, and his new assignments not only paid him better wages, eight dollars a month, but also allowed him to do hard physical work on a number of farms. Jim enjoyed and learned from these off-campus assignments. When he returned to full-time study at the school in 1906, he was ready to settle down in the program in tailoring which was the trade he had selected two years earlier.

During his absence from the campus, much had changed. New programs and buildings had been added, and the school, like Jim himself, had almost reached full growth. Jim was six feet tall, and weighed about 185 pounds. The school now had about 1,100 students, from 87 tribes, living on the 311-acre campus. Aided by its most famous athlete, the Carlisle Indian School was about to enter its greatest period.

By 1906, in addition to its varsity and reserve squads, the school had developed a fine intramural football league, made up of teams from the various trade programs on the campus. The competition was fierce in these games, and it was not at all uncommon for an exceptional performer to move up to one of the school teams. That is what happened to Jim. In one of his first games with the tailors' team, on which he played guard, he caught the eye of the coach of the reserve team. Jim accepted the coach's invitation to complete the season with the Hotshots, the campus name for the reserves.

Early the following year, Jim met the varsity football and track coach — Glen Scobie "Pop" Warner — who was to guide him during the rest of his Carlisle career. During his stay at Carlisle, Pop had enjoyed unusual coaching success. His track teams of 1899 through 1903 had won most of their meets and his football squads of the same period had brought in a 39-18-3 record. But even better seasons lay ahead, thanks especially to the muscular Indian he first saw on the sidelines at the school track late in the spring of 1907.

It was a chance meeting. Jim had been assigned to help clean up around the high-jump areas. While taking a break from his chores, he noticed that all the varsity jumpers were having trouble clearing the bar when it was set at 9 inches over the 5-foot mark. Seven inches above 5 feet was the best that any of them could jump, and just as they were about to give up on the higher level, Jim asked whether he might try. The jumpers, like their coach, were stunned. Why, this fellow was assigned to work detail and was dressed in overalls and tennis shoes. How could he hope to out-jump well-conditioned and warmed-up varsity stars? But since the cocky youngster's attempt would probably provide them all with a good laugh, they allowed him to try. Jim positioned himself about ten feet from the bar, glanced at it quickly, and took off like a flash. The leap amazed them, for Jim had cleared the bar with room to spare. It took several seconds for Pop to believe what he had seen, but as soon as he was himself again, he asked Jim to join the squad for the few remaining weeks of the season. Jim agreed, and his track career at Carlisle had begun.

Pop discovered Jim's football abilities in pretty much the same way. One day, his newest track star happened to pass the varsity football practice field on his way back to his dormitory room. He had been working on one of the campus farms, and he was dressed in work clothes and plow shoes. Jim paused for a few minutes of fun kicking stray footballs which he found lying around the area, and Pop noticed the tremendous distances the kicks traveled. He knew that the varsity could put such talent to good use, and invited him to join the team. Again Jim agreed.

During the four years they were together at Carlisle, Pop and Jim understood and respected each other. Jim liked the knowledge and experience Pop possessed, as well as his ability to handle players. Pop, in turn, respected both Jim's athletic ability and his many fine human qualities. He recognized that his young star had a potential and a personality that needed only to be developed. The two never made impossible demands on one another, but each always knew he could rely on the other.

Even long after he left Carlisle in 1915, Pop claimed that his 1907 football team was his best ever. Two-time All-American back Frank Mt. Pleasant and end A. A. Exendine, who was later a member of the Carlisle coaching staff and the National Football Foundation Hall of Fame, were just two of his many stars. When their skills were joined with those of performers like William Gardner, as a pass-catcher surpassed only by Exendine, and Pete Hauser, one of the greatest runners and kickers Pop ever coached, there was no stopping the team.

That year, Jim performed only as a substitute halfback. Pop was preparing him for the gridiron greatness he could see was possible in the youngster, and he placed him on the bench just often enough to make him eager to play his best in future seasons. Jim did not like to watch competition; he liked to be a part of it. After the 1907 season, he vowed he would be right in the middle of all that he could handle.

And he was. During later Carlisle competitions, in track as well as football, he didn't sit still very often. With the help of Pop, Jim soon became skilled in many track activities. He liked them all, and the more events he tried, the more he mastered, and the more medals he won. Running, high-jumping, pole-vaulting, hurdling, discus-throwing — all were easy for him. Medals followed medals, success followed success. By 1909, he was almost a one-man track team.

And in meets that year with two large schools, he proved his ability. With just four teammates, he led Carlisle to a 71-to-31 victory over a forty-six-man squad from powerful Lafayette. Later, he and only seven others traveled to Syracuse to take on and defeat that university's team of about fifty athletes.

In football he enjoyed similar success. The 1908 season found him playing at left halfback, and sensational runs and kicks became almost as commonplace as track medals. The team recorded 10 wins and a tie in 13 games with some of the country's finest football powers. When playing

Harvard, Jim made the game's most spectacular run, traveling 65 yards. Against Penn State he kicked 3 field goals, all the points the Indians needed for the win. Jim's fine performances did not go unnoticed, and shortly after season's end, he was offered a third-team spot on Walter Camp's All-American Team.

But the Carlisle Indian School was not only athletic activities. It was also books, studies, chores, and off-campus work. After the 1909 track season, and before Jim could try to repeat or outdo his football feats of 1908, he had to go out again to work in some paying job. Although he had not disliked employment on the Pennsylvania farms, this time he wanted to make his money doing something athletic. He mentioned his idea to several of the school's baseball players with whom he had sometimes played after his track activities. It took little argument from them to convince him that he should try out for the Rocky Mount baseball team, which was in the Eastern Carolina League. Jim always loved a challenge, and he quickly packed his bags and hurried to North Carolina, where he made the team. The pay was small, but Jim did not care. All he valued was the chance to compete and to have fun.

Unlike all the other players in the league, Jim had played little college baseball, for he was too busy in track events to get a real chance at the sport. But he became one of the team's star performers. He enjoyed the game so much that he remained in Rocky Mount until mid-season of 1910, when he moved to the Fayetteville team of the same league.

As a hitter, he averaged about .250 during his two North Carolina seasons, a surprising figure for one who had not played much baseball. Even more amazing, however, were his mound and baserunning accomplishments. His blazing fast ball gave the team 19 pitching victories, and his natural speed was responsible for many stolen bases and runs. Because he always gave them a good show, regardless of where he was playing on the diamond, the fans loved him and flocked to see him perform.

Jim was also quite a performer away from the playing field. He liked to compete even when out of uniform. One morning, as he was sitting in restaurant on Hay Street in Fayetteville, he made a bet that almost got him killed. After breakfast he still had about an hour before leaving by train for a game. Jim decided to bet a companion five dollars that he could successfully jump through the window of the restaurant in which they were sitting. He promised that although the glass would shatter into a thousand pieces, he would land unhurt and on his feet on the sidewalk outside. His friend had never heard of such an incredible feat, and he quickly accepted. Jim, without a blink of his eyes, took off for his target. Turning as he dived toward the huge window, he allowed his powerful back and shoulders to take the blow as he exploded through the glass and onto the pavement. His landing was perfect, and once his feet hit the cement sidewalk, they never lost their balance. Jim had won his bet.

As Jim placed the five dollars in his pants pocket, a spectator pushed forward through the crowd. He believed he had seen a once-in-a-lifetime happening, and bet Jim a second five-dollar bill that he could not repeat the trick. Jim told the stranger that he would be happy to win more money. Together, they marched down the block to the Clark Grocery Store, whose front window was just as large as the restaurant glass that Jim had destroyed. The store owner was impressed by Jim's window-breaking skill, but quickly warned him that he should not try it in his place of business. His front window was too expensive to be easily replaced. But Jim, feeling in the mood for some fun, refused to take no for an answer. He proceeded to the rear of the store, where he planned to begin his dash for the glass. The owner repeated his warning but Jim, with a playful grin on his face, paid no attention. Since Jim would not listen, the owner decided that he must resort to violence to keep his window in one piece. Grabbing an ax handle on sale in his store, he went to stand only a few feet from the window that Jim was going to shatter in his dive for the street outside. As Jim raced by him, the owner landed a knock-out blow on Jim's skull.

Quickly, several bystanders gathered up Jim's motionless body and carried it to Dr. J. H. Marsh's office, just a few doors from the Clark store. Dr. Marsh put eight stitches in Jim's head and wrapped it in a mass of bandages. He allowed Jim, still dazed from the blow, to head for the Fayetteville Railroad Station. Several hours later, with bandages sticking out from under his baseball cap, Jim went out on the playing field — and much to the amazement of the fans in the stands, played an excellent game.

Curiously, it was an injury on the baseball diamond that kept Jim from finishing the 1910 season in Fayetteville. Long after his window-breaking attempt, he badly strained his throwing and pitching arm. One morning, he found that he could hardly lift it, much less play baseball with it. He decided that he needed a long rest and that the best place for that was Oklahoma. Besides, he was anxious to see relatives and old friends once again. So he returned to his native state after an absence of several years. He enjoyed his trip west, and, even more, he enjoyed revisiting places and people he had known in times past.

Most of all, he enjoyed the letter that reached him there in the spring of 1911. Pop Warner wanted him back at Carlisle. His teammates, his teachers, the townspeople — everyone missed him. There were a lot of tough athletic contests ahead for the Carlisle team, his coach pointed out, and Jim could play a part, a big part, if he decided to continue his education. Jim was convinced — he had been away from sports and studies long enough. He missed Carlisle, and he decided it was time to return.

1912 Carlisle football team,
Jim and Pop Warner in the center of the back row

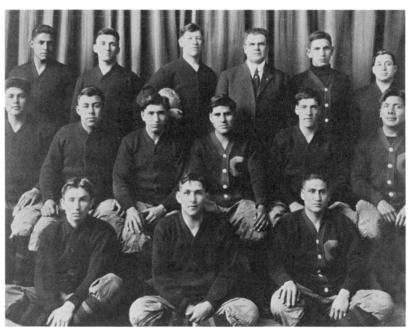

And what a return it was! His athletic accomplishments went from great to amazing. No other gridiron performer has ever enjoyed two better campaigns than those he played in 1911 and 1912. Walter Camp, in choosing the All-Americans, had no choice whatever in placing him on the first team in both 1911 and 1912.

In 1911, the Carlisle team captured 11 of 12 contests. The lone loss, by 1 point, came at the hands of Syracuse because of Carlisle's overconfidence. Jim played a major role in almost every game, as the Indians recorded triumph after triumph over the nation's best football schools. Against Dickinson, he scored 17 points in 17 minutes. Against Lafayette, he lofted a punt more than 70 yards. Against Brown, he got even greater distance on a kick — 83 yards, a new Andrews Field record. And against Harvard, in his most magnificent game of the season, he made all of Carlisle's points by scoring a touchdown on a 70-yard run and by booting 4 field goals, the longest from the 48-yard line.

His 1912 season was even more spectacular. As captain of the Indians, he led them to 12 wins and a tie in 14 games. He scored 198 points, a single-season total that no player, past or present, has ever surpassed. Against Pittsburgh, he sent a punt 70 yards, kicked 6 conversions, and scored 28 of his team's 45 points. Against Dickinson, after grabbing a bad pass from center, he ran the length of the field — and then calmly added the extra point. Against Army, whose left halfback Dwight "Ike" Eisenhower was later to become President of the United States, Jim scored 22 of Carlisle's 27 points. On consecutive runs in this game, the first of them called back because of a penalty, he raced 189 yards. After the Brown game, the referee admitted:

I've just officiated at a game in which I've seen the greatest football player ever. Jim Thorpe defeated Brown thirty-two to nothing, all by himself. Runs of fifty and sixty yards were nothing, the Indian was a tornado. He wrecked the entire Brown team.

In spite of his success these two seasons, Jim remained generous and even tempered. J. C. Oxendine, who attended Carlisle with Jim at the height of Jim's success, said that he never once saw him lose his temper, on or off the playing field. He was "an easy fellow to get along with." Jim now was receiving one-fourth to one-third of all the letters sent to the students, but he did not let his success spoil him.

Jim's teachers during that period shared the same opinion. "James Thorpe was always helpful, always chivalrous and kindly. . . . [He was] an exceedingly generous boy." So spoke Marianne Moore, who taught at Carlisle and later became one of America's most respected poets. She said, "I was fond of him. . . . 'Miss Moore, may I carry your parasol?' That was the way he was."

During this two-year period, too, Jim found time for many sports besides football. Boxing, wrestling, lacrosse, gymnastics, swimming, hockey, handball, basketball — Jim participated and did well in them all. He was, of course, excellent in football. But not even this was his strongest activity. During this period, it was in track and field that he performed best. It was in track and field, in far-off Sweden during the summer of 1912, that he proved, to the amazement of the entire world, that he was indeed the finest athlete who ever lived.

CHAPTER III

The
Olympics

Every four years, nations from all over the globe send their finest athletes to compete for international honors. The Olympic Games attract only the best in each field, and only a few of these ever succeed. Most return to their native lands happy for the experience but without a medal. The handful who do win are true champions.

During the summer of 1912, in Stockholm, Jim did what no one else has ever been able to do: he won both the pentathlon and the decathlon, the two most trying events of the Olympic Games.

Only athletes gifted with a variety of skills can hope to do well in either event. The pentathlon demands excellence in five areas: the running broad jump, the javelin throw, the 200-meter run, the 1500-meter run, and the discus throw. The decathlon calls for even greater skill and strength. It includes the 100-meter dash, the 110-meter high hurdles, the 400-meter run, the 1500-meter run, the discus throw, the javelin throw, the shot put, the broad jump, the high jump, and the pole vault. These are all heavy demands, but for Jim, the events were simply good competition and fun.

The story of his participation in the Olympics actually

began more than a year before he ever set foot in Sweden. In the letter that reached Jim in Oklahoma in the spring of 1911, Pop Warner asked him to think about entering the international contests that were coming up. Pop said that he would be happy to help train his star athlete. Jim liked the idea of traveling abroad and testing his talents against the best other countries had to offer. And he was happy to prepare under the watchful eye of Pop.

But preparation for Jim was not what it is for most athletes. He needed only a short period to work himself into top shape, and then he could stay sharp simply by competing, concentrating, and relaxing. Here is Jim's description of the unusual training program that he found perfect for competition:

> Two or three weeks will put anyone in perfect condition if he is willing to work out properly. My own system at Carlisle was to go out on a few warm days, jog and exercise for two or three hours in the morning under a hot sun in heavy sweat clothes, come in and take a nap, and then go back in the afternoon and repeat the performance. During this period I did not eat very much food and drank practically no water.
>
> In a few days' time I found myself right.

To stay "right," Jim added, all you have to do is get plenty of rest and "know what you are going to do before you do it, and then act."

But in Jim's time, most coaches did not respect rest and concentration as much as he did. They believed that to remain in shape an athlete had to work out day after day, week after week. On the ocean liner that took him across the Atlantic, Jim ran into trouble with the coach of the Olympic squad. Coach Mike Murphy realized Jim possessed unusual track and field abilities. He had seen Jim high-jump 6 feet, 5 inches, just ⅝ of an inch below the world record at that time. However, he could not believe that the Carlisle star could train by lying in a hammock. He kept his eye on Jim, but he never saw him move a muscle, except to measure off distances on the ship's deck, study them carefully, and then lie back down for another nap. Finally the coach could remain silent no longer. He stormed up to Pop and shouted, "Glen, I've seen some queer birds in my day but your Indian beats all. I don't see him do anything except sleep."

Pop was aware of Jim's routine, and he approved of it. He thought for a moment before telling Coach Murphy not to worry. "All those two-for-a-nickel events you've got lined up for Thorpe won't bother him. He's in shape. What with football, lacrosse, baseball, and track back at school, how could he be out of shape? This sleeping is the best training ever, for Jim."

And it was. On July 6, 1912, the first day of the Games, Jim easily captured the pentathlon. He was so much better than his competition that he won first place in 4 of the 5 events, taking third place in the javelin throw. The athlete who finished behind him (F. R. Bie, a Norwegian) was totally overpowered. In short, the pentathlon was, as one writer described it, "no contest at all . . . just as easy for Jim as picking strawberries out of a dish."

The decathlon nine days later was not much more difficult for him. He finished in first place in 4 events, in third place in 4 others, and in fourth place in 2: the 400-meter run and the javelin throw. The athlete who finished second

Jim in the shot-put portion of the Decathlon event

King Gustav presenting Jim the Pentathlon trophy

(Hugo Wieslander, from Sweden) earned only 7,724.495 points, while Jim's total was almost 700 higher: 8,412.96 points.

Another reason why Jim's Olympic victories were so amazing is the fact that he competed in borrowed track shoes. Just minutes before the 200-meter race was to begin, Jim could not find his favorite spikes. Pop was frantic. He knew Jim was no ordinary person, but he thought that even Jim couldn't win unless he wore comfortable shoes. But Jim quickly restored his coach's faith. After trying on and lacing up a pair of shoes that happened to be lying unclaimed near the track, he assured Pop that he was ready for competition — and the performances that followed proved he was.

Two easy wins in the two most demanding of Olympic activities! King Gustav of Sweden said, as he presented Jim with the two magnificent trophies, "Sir, you are the greatest athlete in the world." The entire world was amazed, but everyone agreed with King Gustav. And Jim was never to forget those words.

CHAPTER IV

Professional Baseball

It was the end of January when word reached Pop that Jim might have to give up his Olympic awards. Several days earlier a newspaper in the East had carried a note on Jim's days in Rocky Mount and Fayetteville. The secretary of the Amateur Athletic Union had immediately asked Pop to help check the story. If Jim had once played baseball for pay, then he had not been an amateur when participating in the Olympic Games of the previous year. Jim might lose the trophies he had won in Sweden.

Jim was stunned and confused, but he denied nothing. He explained that he had indeed played Eastern Carolina League baseball, but definitely not for the money that he had gained. Since off-campus work was a big part of the Carlisle program, he had decided after the 1909 track season to get a job playing sports rather than working on farms. Just as before, he had simply been earning money to help with his school expenses. And he had never tried to hide anything from anyone. Many other college players in the Eastern Carolina League at that time had played using phony names, but "James Francis Thorpe" was the name that had appeared in the box scores of both North Carolina cities.

He could not understand why the A.A.U. had suddenly decided to check on his baseball of years past. After all, he pointed out to Pop, dozens of professional baseball's talent scouts had watched him perform without ever thinking of him as anything but a college athlete. Fans and sportswriters who had seen him play in Rocky Mount and Fayetteville and then watched him in the Olympics had never questioned his amateur status. He remembered, too, that at no time during his stay in the Carolinas had he signed a contract. How could he have been a professional, he asked, without ever putting his signature on a legal contract?

Jim struggled hard to explain why he was guilty of no wrongdoing. Pop listened to Jim and then promised to do all within his power to help him. He immediately began a long letter to the A.A.U. secretary defending Jim's participation in the Olympics.

A few days later, Jim prepared his own letter to A.A.U. officials. He said that he had played Carolina baseball only because he enjoyed the game. In his own heart, he believed himself to be an amateur in 1909 and 1910, as well as at the Olympic tryouts, the Stockholm contests, and right up to the present moment.

On the same teams I played with were several college men from the North who were earning money by ball playing during their vacations and were regarded as amateurs at home. I did not play for the money there was in it, because my property brings me in enough money to live on, but because I like to play ball.

I was not very wise to the ways of the world and did not realize that this was wrong and it made me a pro-

fessional in track sports. . . . I hope I will be partly
excused by the fact that I was simply an Indian school
boy and did not know that I was doing wrong because
I was doing what I knew several college men had
done, except that they did not use their own names.

Many famous sportswriters came to his defense, too. But
the A.A.U. took a different view. They argued that "we
had no choice but to declare him a professional" and to
demand the return of all the Olympic awards. No amount
of protesting could save what Jim had earned — not Jim's
pleas, not those of Pop or important sportswriters or influ-
ential American citizens. Jim's name and point totals must
be removed from the Olympic record book, and his medals
and trophies must be returned to Sweden.

It was a sad day in February, 1913, when Jim and Pop
packaged the gold medals and huge trophies and carried
them to the Carlisle post office. The medals would be given
to the men who had finished second to Jim in the two
Olympic events.

But neither F. R. Bie of Norway, who finished second
in the pentathlon, nor Hugo Wieslander of Sweden, who
was second in the decathlon, saw himself as a 1912 Olympic winner. Both knew they had been runners-up, and they
refused the medals that Jim had won just a few months
earlier. Mr. Wieslander never even opened the box with his
name on it. He simply sent the package back to the Olympic Committee with this note: "I didn't win the Olympic
decathlon. James Thorpe did. I don't know what your rules
are in regard to amateurism, but I do know, having competed against him, that Thorpe is the greatest athlete in the
world."

Years later, Jim stated that his biggest thrill as an athlete came when he learned that Hugo Wieslander had sent back the unopened box containing his decathlon medal. Jim always respected the noble actions of his opponents. He was grateful that they realized, even if A.A.U. and Olympic Committee officials did not, that he had truly won in Stockholm.

"The act that barred Thorpe could never be justified," commented sportswriter Grantland Rice. Jim knew he had been cheated but he did not allow his disappointment to make him a bitter man. He was approaching his twenty-fifth birthday and his prime of life, and he knew that there was too much playing ahead for him to worry about injustice or unfairness. He was the world's best-known athlete, and he was confident that he could use this fame and his natural ability to help him succeed as a professional baseball player. After all, he decided, since some people had already called him a professional, he might just as well become one. And several major-league teams had shown an interest in signing him to a contract. Although he viewed baseball as one of his weakest sports (and one that he had not really played in three years), he believed he could succeed in it if he gave it real time and attention.

The Chicago White Sox, the St. Louis Browns, the Cincinnati Reds, and the Pittsburgh Pirates all wanted his services. That February, just weeks before the start of spring training, the four teams sent representatives to Carlisle to make him an offer. But Jim wanted to play with the best, and he rejected all four opportunities, even though two of the scouts stayed an entire week at Carlisle trying to get him to change his mind. It was the New York Giants, champions of the National League in both 1911 and 1912, who signed Jim to a three-year contract at $6,000 a year. This was the club Jim respected most.

Many newspapers throughout the country praised his decision. The *New York Times* was especially happy with it, for they believed the Giants had won the services of a player with a great deal of potential and "drawing power." Jim could help the team both on the field and at the gate.

His decision was very important to someone else, too — a girl named Iva Margaret Miller. Like Jim, she was an Oklahoma native, and she had transferred to Carlisle from the Chilocco Indian School. Shortly after arriving in Pennsylvania, she began dating Jim. He was still feeling the loss of Big Hiram, and found her to be a quiet but understanding companion, a girl who could be comfortable with a loner. During Jim's rise to fame, she proved to be a true friend, and was always willing to answer Jim's questions or give sound advice. The contract with the Giants gave him the money that he knew he needed for marriage. So Jim and Iva, deeply in love, planned a post-season wedding in St. Patrick's Catholic Church in Carlisle.

Jim's future seemed very bright as he went to Marlin, Texas, for spring training with his new team. Immediately, he proved he could run and throw with any major league outfielder, and his batting looked powerful and promising. On his first trip to the plate against Christy Mathewson, the best pitcher on the New York team and perhaps the best pitcher ever to appear in the big leagues, Jim hit Mathewson's famous pitch, his "fadeaway," over the left field fence. The blow so impressed Giant manager John McGraw that he later called it "the hardest ball that ever was hit." In March of 1913, Jim was making a good start in his baseball career, and it seemed to be only a matter of time before he would prove to be one of the game's stars.

But although he was not aware of them at the time, Jim had two strikes against him from the beginning. The first was Manager McGraw, the "Little Napoleon" of baseball. McGraw kept tight controls on his players, and he demanded their complete respect. He was no Pop Warner. He did not try to get along with his players; he wished only to command them and shape them into a first-rate team.

The second handicap was Jim's unusual training routine. It had already gotten him into trouble with Coach Murphy of the Olympic squad, and it was bound to get him into trouble with McGraw, who believed that all baseball players had to practice and play hard every day of spring training and the championship season. He had never coached, or even heard of, a successful player who spent so much time concentrating and resting. He was not about to accept one at this point in his managing career.

The personality conflict between Jim and his manager grew worse once the regular season began. Neither man would give an inch. Neither planned to change his ways. Despite Jim's fine showing in Texas, McGraw did not place him in the lineup until the middle of May — and then only as a pinch hitter in the ninth inning of a game with the Pittsburgh Pirates.

Jim hated sitting on the bench, playing only a game here and a game there. He had hated it at Carlisle during the football season of 1907, and he hated it even more now because he felt he could help the Giants as a regular outfielder. But McGraw disagreed. He seemed more interested in breaking Jim's spirit than in developing his potential. Finally, after a close game that New York lost, the two men clashed in the team clubhouse. They shouted angry words at each other, and Jim lunged for McGraw. The two had to be separated by other players.

Jim had ruined his chances to play with the Giants in the 1913 season. Within twenty-four hours, he received word to report to Toledo, in the International League. He was stuck out there while New York went on to win its third straight pennant. After the World Series, which the

Batting for the New York Giants in 1914

Giants lost to the Philadelphia Athletics in 5 games, Jim was invited to rejoin the team for a baseball tour of the world. He was happy to accept and to forget, at least for a few weeks, his trouble with McGraw. Jim especially enjoyed the trip, because just before leaving the United States, he and Iva married, and the tour gave them a lengthy, exciting honeymoon.

But the three seasons that followed proved no more rewarding for Jim than his first one. Both 1914 and 1915 he spent mainly in the minor leagues, playing only 47 games in a New York uniform. During the 1916 season, he did not appear with the Giants even once. McGraw told the sportswriters who constantly asked about Jim that the reason he could not play in the big leagues was curve balls, which, McGraw said, were a big problem for him at the plate. But the real reason was not Jim's playing ability. McGraw still wanted to control him, and Jim enjoyed his own way of playing and relaxing too much to give in to the "Little Napoleon." Each had his own strong style and personality, and neither was about to change for the other.

Thus, although his future had seemed promising, Jim's first four professional seasons were not outstanding. It seemed that he was about to experience his first athletic failure ever. But the six seasons that followed proved that he really did have fine baseball ability. He spent all of the 1917, 1918, and 1919 seasons in the National League, and each year managed to improve his batting average. He hit .237 in 1917, .248 the next year, and .327 in 1919, his last season in the majors. The next three campaigns he spent in the high minor leagues, and each one was successful. At Akron in the International League in 1920, he hit a powerful .360, stole 22 bases, and hammered 16 home runs. At Toledo in the American Association the next year, he hit just 2 points below his Akron average while stealing 34 bases and knocking in 112 runs. And splitting his time between the Pacific Coast League and the Eastern League in 1922, his final professional baseball season, he hit for a .335 average and stole 24 bases.

Between 1917 and 1922 Jim proved that his differences with McGraw, not curve balls, had kept him from major-league stardom. He had the physical tools necessary for success. If only the New York manager had worked with him and tried to develop his skills, Jim probably would have a place today in baseball's Hall of Fame. After his retirement from the sport, Jim proudly reported, "I could hit any kind of a ball from any kind of a pitcher."

Added to his troubles with the "Little Napoleon" during his baseball career was a personal loss which he suffered in 1918. His infant son, Jim, caught the flu, and even the best medicines and doctors in New York City could not save him. Jim and Iva's first child had carried not only his father's name but also his hopes for great athletic success. Jim believed the boy might one day regain the Olympic awards that had been taken from his father. But the four-year-old's tragic death ended those hopes, and once again Jim mourned in silence. He disappeared from Iva and the Giants for several days — not even McGraw could find him — and he shared his grief with no one. Then suddenly he was back in New York and in uniform once again, pretending that nothing had happened and ready to continue his baseball career.

Something had happened to him, however. Eleven years

later he was heard to say that the death of his young son marked the beginning of his athletic decline, the beginning of the end for him as an athlete.

But in 1918 no one suspected as much. After burying the boy in Oklahoma soil not far from his other loved ones, Jim continued on with the best years of his baseball career. And in 1922, after ten years as a professional baseball player and after four straight seasons of hitting over .300, he decided that it was time to give his full attention to another professional sport. Football, which he loved even more than baseball, wanted Jim, and he could not resist.

CHAPTER V

Professional
Football

Jim started to play professional football in 1915, when he was still drawing crowds at the baseball field. At that time, professional football was very different from what it is today. Fans today know, for instance, that the equipment is the finest, and that the players are all paid well for this rough sport. But at the turn of the century, fans thought differently, and for good reason. They realized that professional football was simply an infant who, if nursed carefully, might go on to see a better day. They knew professional football needed a great deal of help. Interested and wealthy team owners were a must. So were faithful fans. And great college players had to agree to give their gridiron best after graduation, even though professional football was much rougher than the college game and the pay was very small.

Jim supplied one of those helping hands, perhaps the most important one of all. He played the game for fifteen years, and for fifteen years he was the best. Even as he approached forty years of age, and after, team owners were anxious to gamble on him with a contract. They knew that, old or young, he could play the game with the toughest graduates of the nation's leading football schools.

Teammates were just as confident. They knew that "Indian Jim," as sportswriters were fond of calling him, could lead them to victory over even the best opponents. Fans, too, had faith in him. They were willing to pay the price of a ticket because they knew he would not disappoint them with his running, passing, kicking, and tackling. Jim was truly the first of the great names that were to make professional football the tremendous success it is today.

But back in 1915, when Jim was starting his career, only one man had real faith that he could jump from college football to the pro game. Jack Cusack was the owner of the Canton, Ohio, Bulldogs, and he was confident that Jim could lead his team to professional greatness. Against the wishes of his advisors, who believed that Jim's salary would put the team into bankruptcy, Jack agreed to pay Jim the unheard-of sum of $250 a game. No other player was earning such big money, and Jack's advisors didn't believe that Thorpe was worth the risk. They felt he would prove to be a failure in the pro game, the Bulldogs would get in financial trouble, and the team would probably fold.

But the owner would not bend. Jim deserved the money, he told them, because the great college athlete could be even greater as a professional. And Cusack proved to be correct. Jim led Canton to a tie for the professional championship in his first season and to an undisputed title in 1916. More important, right away he was the sport's top gate attraction. People flocked to the parks to watch him perform. Cusack explained that "all the fans wanted to see the big Indian in action."

And seldom did Jim disappoint them. He led Canton to

consistent success for six seasons. He once boomed a punt an unbelievable 90 yards; and against Indianapolis a short time later, he drop-kicked a field goal an amazing 75 yards.

Off the field he was just as important in helping the young sport. Although he was playing professional baseball as well as professional football, he still found time in 1920 to serve as the first president of the American Professional Football Association (APFA), the league that today is known as the National Football League. Jim was far too busy for the important assignment, but he agreed to be elected to it. He knew that the eleven-team league could survive only if people who loved the game gave it their every effort. He also knew that the team owners were relying on him for leadership. He was the game's biggest name, the owners pointed out to him, so he was the only man for the demanding job.

With Cusack as his business manager, Jim moved on to the Cleveland Indians of the APFA in 1921. Together they brought the team success on the gridiron as well as at the gate. In 1922, he switched to the Rock Island Independents, and after three fine seasons with them, he returned to New York to play with the powerful professional football Giants. Later in 1925, it was back to Rock Island, and still later in the same season he appeared with the St. Petersburg, Florida, professional club.

Along the way, Jim even found time to organize and to play on his own team. Years later he proudly said that the Oorang Indians, of LaRue, Ohio, were the finest professional football team he ever performed with. Small wonder, of course. The game's greatest player not only was a member of the squad but he also managed to coax other out-

standing Indian players to join him. From Haskell Institute came Red Fox, a first-rate quarterback; and from
Carlisle came gridiron greats like back Joe Guyon and
lineman Elmer Busch, an All-American in 1913. Jim's
former teammates were happy to play with him once again.
And even happier were young Indians from the far corners
of the United States who were invited to play by his side.
The Oorang Indians, made up entirely of American Indians, were "a team to strike terror in any squad that
opposed it," as one sportswriter described Jim's hand-
picked crew.

Jim's football travels, however, were not always fun
filled. There were disappointments, too. In 1923, Iva tired
of his heavy schedule and constant moving, and she divorced him. After the tragic death of Jim, Jr., five years
earlier, the couple had drifted farther and farther apart.
Three other children had later been born to them, each a
beautiful, healthy girl and a joy to her parents. But Jim's
athletic career allowed him little time to spend with them
and their mother, and finally he agreed to the divorce. He
and Iva remained good friends in later years, but after
1923, their lives took different directions.

Painful, too, was Jim's growing belief that retirement
from the game he loved most was fast approaching. He
realized that time would soon catch up with him. Jim hated
the thought of leaving the athletic field, but he knew that
he was not getting better, only older, slower, and less agile.
Each tackle took just a bit more out of him. Years earlier,
he had learned to pace himself on the gridiron, to save his
best for the most important plays and moments of a contest. But even pacing would not allow him to play forever,

Jim and one of his children

he realized. Retirement would have to come.

And it did. At the age of thirty-seven, Jim announced to the world that he would never play again. He wanted to retire to his native Oklahoma and to spend his time with his old friends there — "to hunt and fish with them." But team owners refused to believe him and they would not take no for an answer. Jim was never good at saying no — not to friends, or even enemies, and certainly not to men who wanted him to continue in the game that had been such an important part of his life. So he went on playing, first with the Canton Bulldogs, and later with the Portsmouth, Ohio, professional team, and the Hammond, Indiana, club.

Finally, in 1929, after a season with the Chicago Cardinals, he made up his mind to leave the sport once and for all. At forty-one, his body scarred from the many beating it had taken, but his mind filled with proud memories, Jim quit football for the final time. He had earned a rest. He wanted now to turn his attention to activities that were less demanding physically. With his second wife, Freeda Kirkpatrick Thorpe, whom he had married in 1926, and with a second family to support, he planned to be busy. He wanted to use his talents and energies in a new way.

CHAPTER VI

Ups
and Downs

"Black Tuesday," October 29, 1929, began one of America's worst nightmares. On that day, the stock market crashed as it had never crashed before, and as it has never crashed since. No one escaped the effect of the Great Depression, the worst financial crisis the United States has ever faced. There was little money around, and there were even fewer jobs. Millionaires joined soup lines. Successful businessmen sold apples on street corners. For about a dozen years, until the 1940s, the country fought to stay alive.

The Great Depression was a difficult time for every American, and Jim was no exception. It was certainly a poor time to be seeking a job — and a worse time yet to be switching careers. Jim was trying to do both, and he met with little luck. He went from job to job and from place to place, but nothing really brought him success. At first he tried his hand at painting, a talent that he had developed at Carlisle. He could not make a living at it. Then he became an actor in Hollywood, where he appeared in a number of films as an "extra" or "bit" player. But Hollywood, like the country as a whole, was not enjoying good health, and Jim finally had to seek work elsewhere. In 1931, and several other times after that, he used a pick and shovel as a day laborer. Yet four dollars a day was not much money for a man with a wife and four young sons, and Jim again moved. The times were tough for an ex-athlete who had known so much success in his earlier years.

He worked in Illinois, in Michigan, in Oklahoma. Guard, supervisor of recreation, bartender, master of ceremonies — Jim tried them all, but he was not satisfied with any of them. His marriage, too, was unhappy. In 1943, Freeda wanted the marriage to end, and Jim was divorced a second time. By this time, Jim had a new problem — alcohol — and this was the real cause of Freeda's unhappiness with Jim. He drank too much, she claimed, and the courts agreed.

But Jim refused to believe that things would not get better. "I'll come out of this, you can be sure," he would say. Even in 1943, after he suffered his first heart attack, those words were on his lips. He wanted pity from no one. He had faith in himself. Life would surely be better in the future.

And occasionally it was. At the 1932 Olympic Games, held in California, he shared the Presidential box with another Indian who had made a success of his life: Charles Curtis, Vice-President of the United States. At the urging of the crowd, Jim stood while they gave him a standing ovation. Fans from across the world had not forgotten. Jim was still their hero.

Five years later, Jim was once again remembered by citizens from many lands. He led a movement to regain certain rights for his people, the Sac and Fox tribe of

Oklahoma. The movement did not succeed, but Jim had fought bravely for it, and even opponents respected him for his fine efforts. They knew he had given countless hours to the cause and had spent a great deal of money trying to help his tribe. It was impossible to have anything but respect for so generous and sincere a man.

And although the years flew by, Jim still had athletic skill. At age fifty, he won over a hundred dollars for a friend because of his jumping ability. The friend had bet a bunch of young college athletes that an old man he knew could beat any and all of them in the standing broad jump. The college boys were delighted, for they were sure that no fifty-year-old could top their best efforts. But they did not know that their opponent was Jim Thorpe. After stretching his legs a couple of times, Jim showed them the form and ability that had made him famous. He jumped 10 feet, 8 inches — only 6 inches behind the world record.

Seven years later the United States was at war, and Jim wanted to do his part. He tried to enlist, but no branch of the service would have him. The Army, the Navy, and the Marines all told him that he was too old to help. But Jim kept trying. Finally, the Merchant Marines accepted him, and during the war Jim sailed the high seas on a cargo ship that carried live explosives to far-off India. It was a dangerous job, but Jim was proud because he helped his country in its time of need.

In 1945, he married for the third time. Shortly before his enlistment in the Merchant Marines, Jim wed Patricia Askew of Louisville, Kentucky. He had met her over twenty years earlier when he was playing with the Rock Island Independents. Through the years, although they never saw each other, she remained a fan of his. A chance meeting in California early in 1945 brought the pair together a second time, and the friendship very quickly turned into a lasting relationship.

The new Mrs. Thorpe was a capable businesswoman, and she was able to help him handle and save money. She urged Jim to continue to be generous, but she would not let him be so free with his earnings that he failed to provide for himself. As 1950 approached, it seemed that Jim's luck was about to change for the better.

CHAPTER VII

The Last
Years

At important times in their history, people like to look back and judge what has been accomplished so far, and see who has accomplished it. In 1950, many Americans took a look back over the first half-century. This was a time for identifying the important and the great — the "best of them all" in each of hundreds of fields.

Football players did not escape the people's notice, for the past fifty years had produced hundreds of great grid-iron performers. It should have been difficult to choose the one who was best of all — the greatest football player of the half-century. But it was not. Jim won easily. In an Associated Press poll, sportswriters and broadcasters from each state made their selections, and Jim won hands down. He collected 170 votes, 32 more than the man in second place — college and professional backfield star Harold "Red" Grange, the "Galloping Ghost." In third place, over 130 votes behind Jim, was the great Bronco Nagurski, who had been so good in college football that he had won All-American honors at not one but two positions, tackle and halfback. Jim, however, was the best, and every newspaper in the country made sure every American knew it. In late

January of 1950, Jim was once again his nation's hero.

Jim's fans were anxious to honor and to hear from him. But before he could accept all their invitations, a still greater honor fell to him. The Associated Press had polled sportswriters and announcers a second time, and on February 12, 1950, the results were made public. Jim had been voted the greatest male athlete of the half-century. Out of the 393 ballots cast, Jim's name appeared first on 252. Baseball's famous Babe Ruth of the New York Yankees took second place with just 86 first-place votes. Following Babe were such athletic immortals as Jack Dempsey, the former heavyweight boxing champion of the world; Ty Cobb, with the highest career batting average ever earned in big-league baseball; Joe Louis, the powerful "Brown Bomber" of prize fighting; and Bobby Jones, perhaps the greatest golfer to appear on a course. But Jim topped all of them — and many more — by a wide margin.

Jim felt flattered and grateful. Invitation upon invitation appeared in his mailbox, and he was very happy to be so well known once again. His mind flashed back to Carlisle and Stockholm; he felt that 1950 was much like the old days, the good old days.

While enjoying all the national — and international — attention, he gained even more honors. Later in 1950, he was elected to the Helms Professional Football Hall of Fame. Early the next year, he won a spot in the College Football Hall of Fame. Just a few months later, Hollywood released *Jim Thorpe, All-American,* a film starring Burt Lancaster that told the story of Jim's action-filled life. By arrangement, the picture had its first showings in the two states where Jim had spent so many of his years. It opened

Statue in the Pro-Football Hall of Fame,
Canton, Ohio

JIM THORPE
1888 – 1953

in August of 1951 in both Oklahoma City, Oklahoma, and Carlisle, Pennsylvania. When the film opened in Carlisle, Jim himself was the major attraction.

The day of the showing was warm and clear, and it brought tremendous joy to the man responsible for the huge celebration. Thousands lined the sidewalks of the city that Jim had made famous forty years earlier, as their hero smiled and waved from the back seat of a convertible car which carried him to the city square. There, still circled by well-wishers, Jim was shown a handsome stone with his name in capital letters followed by the words: The Greatest Athlete and Football Player of the First Half of the 20th Century. August 23, 1951 was a great day for Jim, a day he and the entire sports world were truly proud of.

Jim's son Carl, Jim Thorpe, actress Phyllis Thaxter, Governor Fine of Pennsylvania, and General Trudeau. Commandant of the Carlisle Barracks, on August 23, 1951

But bad luck soon returned to Jim's life. That October he learned that he suffered from lip cancer and that he must have surgery. The operation was successful, but it left Jim a sick man — and a penniless one. "We're broke," Jim's wife announced. "Jim has nothing but his name and his memories. He has spent money on his own people and has given it away."

Ten months later, bad luck struck still another time. In August of 1952, while living in Nevada, he suffered his second heart attack. Jim had to give up the small business he operated. Without an income and sicker than he had ever been before, he had good reason for self-pity. Yet he refused to surrender to it. "I'll come out of this, you can be sure," he promised.

Because of poor health, he had to move back to California, where he hoped to regain his strength. He had plans for a comfortable retirement one day, he told friends, and all he needed was some rest before starting to work for his goal.

At dinner in his house trailer on Saturday, March 28, 1953, he talked to Patricia about his hopes for the future. The day had been pleasant, and Jim remarked that his sixty-fifth birthday was just two months away. Suddenly he stopped talking. He grabbed for his chest, a look of pain on his face. He struggled to rise from his chair, but his feet would not hold him and he fell to the floor. Patricia's screams quickly attracted a neighbor, and just minutes later, a fire rescue squad arrived. But no one's efforts could help him. Jim Thorpe was dead.

CHAPTER VIII

The Present

Just outside the town of Jim Thorpe, Pennsylvania, in a small but well-kept park, lie Jim's remains. Marking the spot is a large and impressive tomb. The setting is calm and peaceful, and it resembles much of the land surrounding Jim's Oklahoma birthplace and boyhood home.

Many people have argued that Jim's burial place — in a city he never even visited — is not suitable and that a change is necessary. But his wife Patricia was responsible for the cross-country move from Jim's first resting place in Oklahoma. It was her belief that a city that admired her husband enough to change its name would be an ideal resting place for Jim. Thus she approved the transfer to the city first known as Mauch Chunk, or "Sleeping Bear."

Elsewhere, in Yale, Oklahoma — the only city in which Jim ever owned a home — the residents are in the process of building a five-million-dollar memorial that will carry Jim's name. They have succeeded in getting President Nixon to approve the sale of about one million Jim Thorpe medals, which will provide a huge sum for their building.

They fight still another battle, too. They believe that Jim's athletic successes were so great that there should be a national organization, carrying his name and with offices in every state, to select the nation's outstanding athletes on the high school, college, and professional levels. The people believe strongly in what Jim did for sports in America, and they are anxious to have his name inspire future athletes to greatness.

Finally, most important of all, the people of Yale were the main force behind the decision of the A.A.U., on October 15, 1973, to restore to Jim his amateur standing for the period of 1908 through 1912. That action opened the eyes of people everywhere to the injustice Jim had lived with during the final forty years of his life. It is hoped that the Olympic Committee will soon surrender to the pressure. The awards belong with the Thorpe family, and Jim's name deserves to be returned to the official Olympic record book.

All agree that Jim was an amazing athlete. He was also a fine American and a credit to Indians everywhere. Sportswriter Grantland Rice was correct when he announced that "Jim Thorpe was a very decent human being . . . a gentleman." No higher tribute can be paid to any person. Such a man truly deserves the respect and recognition of all people.

Jim Thorpe's Track and Field Records at Carlisle

100-yard dash (Carlisle)	10 seconds
100-yard dash (practice sprint at Carlisle)	9.8 seconds
120-yard high hurdles	15 seconds
220-yard low hurdles	23.8 seconds
440-yard race	51 seconds
1,500-meter run	4 minutes 40.1 seconds

High jump . . . . 6′ 5″
Pole vault . . . . 10′ 8″
Broad jump . . . . 23′ 6″
Hammer throw . . . . 138 feet
Shot put . . . . 47′ 9″
Javelin . . . . 138 feet
Discus . . . . 125′ 8″

Jim Thorpe's Olympic Records — 1912

Pentathlon

200-meter race - 1st place . . . . 22.9 seconds
1,500-meter race - 1st place . . . . . . 4 minutes 40.8 seconds
Broad jump - 1st place . . . . 23′ 2.7″
Discus - 1st place . . . . 116′ 8.4″
Javelin - 3rd place . . . . 153′ 2.95″

Decathlon

1,500-meter race - 1st place . . . . . . 4 minutes 40.1 seconds
110-meter high hurdles - 1st place . . . . 15.6 seconds
High jump - 1st place . . . . 6′ 1.6″
Shot put - 1st place . . . . 42′ 5.45″
Broad jump - 3rd place . . . . 22′ 2.3″
Pole vault - 3rd place . . . . 10′ 7.95″
Discus - 3rd place . . . . 121′ 3.9″
100-meter race - 3rd place . . . . 11.2 seconds
400-meter race - 4th place . . . . 52.2 seconds
Javelin - 4th place . . . . 149′ 11.2″

Jim Thorpe's Major League Record

	GAMES	AT BAT	HITS	AVERAGE
6 seasons	289	698	176	.252

A native of New Haven, Connecticut,
Dr. R. W. Reising holds degrees from
Michigan State, the University of
Connecticut, and Duke University. At
Duke, on whose coaching staff he served
in 1966-67, his doctoral dissertation
treated sports and literature. A former
high school and college athlete, he
compiled a 106 and 89 win-loss record
as a head coach in intercollegiate baseball,
and in 1969, his final season in athletics,
he guided Furman University to the
championship of the Southern Conference
and a berth in the NCAA playoffs. At
Pembroke State University he teaches
in the Communicative Arts Department
and the American Indian Studies
Department. He is in his nineteenth
year of college and university service.
The writer of numerous articles for
professional journals, he is also one of
the six contributors to *Creative Approaches
to the Teaching of English*: *Secondary,*
edited by R. Baird Shuman of Duke.

*The photographs are reproduced through
the courtesy of the Cumberland County
Historical Society and the Oklahoma
Historical Society.*

BIOGRAPHIES IN
THIS SERIES ARE

Joseph Brant
Crazy Horse
Geronimo
Chief Joseph
King Philip
Osceola
Powhatan
Red Cloud
Sacajawea
Chief Seattle
Sequoyah
Sitting Bull
Tecumseh
William Warren
William Beltz
Robert Bennett
LaDonna Harris
Oscar Howe
Maria Martinez
Billy Mills
George Morrison
Michael Naranjo
Maria Tallchief
James Thorpe
Pablita Velarde
Annie Wauneka